My Favorite Bedtime Stories from The Holy Quran

Teaching Children Stories & Lessons from The Holy Quran

BY THE SINCERE SEEKER KIDS COLLECTION

Disclaimer: Some of the stories in this book end with nations being destroyed, which may be perceived as not suitable for children by some parents. Please read each story in full before reading it to your children.

The Story of Prophet Adam PBUH | Satan Caused them to Eat from the Forbidden Tree

Allah created the first human being, our father, Prophet Adam PBUH. Then He commanded the Angels, including Iblis (Satan), a devout worshipper of Allah at the time, to prostrate before Adam PBUH out of respect. So they all prostrated, except for Iblees, who refused, and he became a disbeliever. Allah, the Glorious, asked Iblis (Satan), *Why didn't you prostrate as I commanded you?* Satan responded *because I am better than him; you created me from fire, and you created him from clay*. Satan was arrogant and thought he shouldn't prostrate before Prophet Adam PBUH because he was better than him.

Then Allah told Iblis, *Get down from here because it is not appropriate for you to be arrogant here--- you are of those humiliated and disgraced.* Iblis asked Allah to give him a more extended time until judgment day. Allah allowed him to stay longer. Satan hated human beings because he thought he had gotten in trouble because of them. He told God that he would wait and ambush human beings, causing us to slip, make mistakes, and do bad things that further us away from the straight path—the path to God. Then Allah said, *Get out of here; whoever follows you amongst them will get punished.*

Allah, the Glorious, told our father, Prophet Adam PBUH, to enter Paradise with our mother Eve, eat and drink whatever they wished, and live happily. They lived there for a long time. Our Creator, Allah the Glorious, instructed Prophet Adam PBUH not to eat from a particular tree. Then Satan whispered to Prophet Adam and Eve, peace be upon them, and tempted them to eat from the tree. He lied and told them they would live forever if they ate from the tree. Prophet Adam and Eve slipped up and ate from the tree. Then God called them, 'Did I not forbid you from that tree and tell you that Satan is your clear enemy?

Prophet Adam and Eve, peace be upon them, immediately regretted eating from the tree and disobeying Allah. They felt pain, sadness, shame, and loneliness. Prophet Adam and Eve, peace be upon them, acknowledged that they had made a mistake without blaming anyone or anything else. They realized that if Allah did not forgive them and have mercy upon them, they would surely be among the losers. They said: We have wronged ourselves, and if You do not forgive us and have mercy upon us, we will surely be among the losers. So, Prophet Adam and Eve, peace be upon them, made a dua to Allah, which Allah had taught them.

Then Allah accepted their repentance, and they returned to the folds of Allah's path and mercy. After that, Allah asked Prophet Adam PBUH to come down to Earth with our mother Eve after being in Paradise for a long time.

The Story of Prophet Noah PBUH | Building His Ship & the Flood

God sent Prophet Noah PBUH to his people, where he preached day and night for 950 years, calling them to worship the one God and follow his commandments. The more he called his people, the further they ran from him. They would put their fingers in their ears and cover their faces when he preached.

His people denied and mocked him, stating that he was nothing special but another human being among them. Prophet Noah PBUH agreed he was only human, but he was sent from God the Glorious with a clear warning. Prophet Noah PBUH told them to repent and ask Allah for forgiveness as He is the All-Forgiving. He said that if they believed in the message and asked Allah for forgiveness, Allah would shower his blessings upon them and bless them with wealth, children, gardens, rivers, and fruits.

Prophet Noah PBUH would ask his people why they disbelieved in Allah when He created them and everything around them? His people were disrespectful and arrogant. In the end, after 950 years of preaching, only 80 people or so believed in his message. After the denial, God instructed Noah to build a ship. As he was building the boat, his people accused him of being a madman for building a boat made of wood and nails on land, nowhere near any water. Soon, water started to gush from the Earth and fall from the sky. God instructed Prophet Noah PBUH to enter the boat with those who believed in the message. He also commanded Prophet Noah PBUH to take a male and female of every animal aboard with him.

Then God caused a great flood, where water gushed from every crack on the Earth, and rain fell from the skies like never before. Prophet Noah PBUH saw his son overwhelmed by the water, so he cried out, pleading with him to board the boat with the believers and leave the non-believers to their fate. However, his son was thinking in terms of this worldly life and did not rely on the trust and Word of God. He replied to his dad that he would go to a mountain where waves could not reach. Prophet Noah PBUH cried out to his son. His son refused. Then he was drowned with the disbelievers and Noah's wife, who also disbelieved.

The flood had cleansed the Earth of idol worshippers and disbelievers. Not a single person who had disbelieved in God remained on Earth. The ship remains intact upon Mount Judi right until today. God has left it as a sign for all of us.

The Young Men of the Cave That Slept for Over 300 Years

The Holy Quran shares a story about a group of righteous young men who believed and worshipped the One True God. They were living in a society that worshipped idols. Because this group of young men refused to take their society's idols as gods, their families and communities expelled them, and their powerful king wanted them killed. The young men tried to flee. They fled to a cave in a mountain without much wealth, food, and resources. They realized they would kill or force them to join idol worship if they found them. As they entered the cave, while scared, they made a dua prayer to Allah, asking Him for His Mercy and to set their affairs straight, make it proper, and find a way out of the ordeal they were in.

The young men discussed how their people could worship idols without evidence showing they were God. Allah, the Almighty, then gifted them with one of his miracles, causing them to fall into a deep sleep in the cave for 309 years, along with their dog that sat in front of the entrance. They were lying down with their eyes open, and Allah caused them to turn from right to left in their sleep. The sun helped preserve their bodies as they slept. When they woke, they discussed how long they had slept. They stated that perhaps we rested for a day or half a day, Allah knows. They were hungry, so they sent one of them to buy some halal food without causing any attention. They did not know it was 309 years later, so there were different people, a different society, and this society did not worship idols.

One of them went down to buy food, wearing clothes worn 300 years ago. The young man from the cave handed his currency coin to the shop owner. The shop owner did not recognize the coin since it was now over 300 years later, and they now used different types of coins. The shop owner said you must have found some treasure. The city's bishop spoke with the young man from the cave and then talked to the rest of the young men in the cave. Allah caused the young men from the cave to die a natural death. This was a sign to the people that God's promise is always true. The people then debated what they should do with their bodies.

The Story of Prophet Jonah PBUH | Swallowed by a Big Fish

Prophet Jonah (Yunus in Arabic) PBUH was a Prophet of God sent to call his people to worship the one and only God, obey God's commandments, and stop their evil doing. After many attempts to convey the message of God to his people, Prophet Yunus PBUH grew frustrated and angry at his people for not believing in the message from God. His people mocked him, were stubborn, rejected his message, and persisted in their disbelief and wrongdoing. Prophet Jonah PBUH warned that punishment would come to them in three days; then, he left his people without instructions or God's permission.

After Prophet Jonah PBUH left his people, a storm started to form from a distance. His people got together and realized what Prophet Jonah PBUH had been warning them about was becoming true and that they would get destroyed like previous nations if they did not believe and follow God's message. So, they believed in the message and abandoned their idols. They realized their mistakes and asked God for forgiveness. Because of this, Allah, the Most-Merciful, spared them from punishment. Allah, the Glorious, guided their hearts.

Prophet Jonan PBUH, not knowing his people finally believed in his message, boarded a ship. The ship then got caught up in a storm that shook it. The people on the ship realized they would drown if they did not empty the ship and lighten the load, so they threw their belongings into the ocean. But that was not enough; the ship kept shaking. Then they realized they needed someone on the ship to jump off so the rest of the people could survive.

So, the people on the ship decided to draw lots; whoever's name was drawn would have to jump off the boat to make the ship lighter. Prophet Jonah PBUH was drawn, but the people decided to try again because he looked like a righteous man and wanted someone else to jump. So, they drew lots twice more, but Prophet Jonah PBUH was chosen repeatedly. Prophet Jonah PBUH understood this was from God, the Almighty. So, he jumped off the ship.

Prophet Jonah PBUH realized his mistake of abandoning his people without the permission of God. After Prophet Yunus PBUH threw himself into the sea, God caused a big fish to swallow Prophet Jonah PBUH without tearing his flesh or breaking his bones. In three layers of darkness - the depth of the night, the darkness of the bottom of the ocean, the darkness of the Whale's belly - Prophet Jonah PBUH, filled with total despair, turned to Allah, prostrated to Him, and cried out to Him, saying *There is no deity except You; exalted are You. Indeed, I have been of the wrongdoers*. Prophet Jonah PBUH acknowledged that Allah is the only deity worthy of worship, then declared the Greatness of Allah, admitted his sin, and took responsibility for his actions. Then, Allah, the Glorious, released him by having the whale spit him on the shore.

Prophet Johan was sick; his skin was peeling from the acid in the whale's belly. He was in a land without trees. God caused a plant to grow and cover Prophet Jonah PBUH with its shade to protect him from the wind and heal him. After Prophet Jonah's health recovered, God commanded him to return to his people. When he returned, he noticed his people were not harmed and that they had submitted to their Lord. Prophet Jonah PBUH was content as his mission had been accomplished.

The Story of Abraham PBUH | Smashing and Destroying Idols

Prophet Abraham PBUH was blessed with knowledge from Allah from a very young age before he was even a Prophet. He knew that idol worship was wrong and evil. Prophet Abraham's father used to carve idols from wood and stone. Prophet Abraham PBUH advised and urged his father to stop worshipping idols and worship the one and only true God, Allah, the Glorious. But his father did not listen and arrogantly continued his ways. Prophet Abraham PBUH told his father that the idols he would make and worship could not benefit nor harm him. His father got fed up and commanded his son, Abraham PBUH, to leave his house or be stoned. Prophet Abraham PBUH responded *Peace be with you, I will ask Allah to forgive you, and I will leave you.*

Prophet Abraham PBUH would prove to the people that idol worship was wrong; he would remind them that only Allah was in control of everything and is the only one that can give life and death, but they rejected his advice and responded, *We worship idols just like our forefathers did, and we will remain devoted to them.* They rejected Prophet Abraham PBUH as he stood against society for truth and justice and had to do it alone, but he knew God was on his side.

On the day of a festival celebration attended by all the people, Prophet Abraham PBUH snuck into the temple where the idols were and smashed them with a sharp ax, except for the largest one. He then hung the ax around the neck of the biggest idol. He wanted to prove to the people that worshipping idols was foolish. If the idols couldn't even help themselves, how can they help others?

When the idol worshippers returned to their temple, they were shocked to see their idols smashed to the ground and began discussing who could have done this. Prophet Abrahams's name came up as they remembered he disapproved of idol worship. They asked Prophet Abraham PBUH if he had done this, and he replied, *Why don't you ask the big idol who did it?* They replied, *You already know that they do not speak!* Then Prophet Abraham PBUH replied, *Why do you worship them if they cannot benefit or harm you? Why don't you think and reason?* They thought, what if we are wrong and Prophet Abraham PBUH is right. But their stubbornness and arrogance got the better, and they continued their evil ways.

They chained Prophet Abraham PBUH and dug a deep pit, filled it with firewood, and ignited it to throw Prophet Abraham PBUH in for what he had done. The fire was so large that they couldn't even get near it. Then Angel Gabriel came down to Prophet Abraham PBUH and asked him, *O Abraham, do you wish for anything?* Prophet Abraham PBUH replied, *Not from you.* He knew all help comes from Allah, and Allah was going to help him and get him out of this.

As they threw Prophet Abraham PBUH into the huge fire, God the Almighty, the All-Powerful, commanded the fire to be cool and safe for Prophet Abraham PBUH. The fire submitted to its Creator. The flames were still there, and the fire burned the chains off. Still, the fire did not burn Prophet Abraham PBUH or feel hot. He was sitting on a fire that turned into a garden—the fire had become cool for him.

The crowd watched the fire from a distance, and the smoke nearly suffocated them. Prophet Abraham PBUH glorified and praised Allah, the Almighty. Prophet Abraham PBUH walked out of the fire peacefully. After this, he migrated to another land with his wife Sara and Hajar to worship Allah. When you place your trust in Allah, He will be enough to get you out of any situation you are in.

The Companion of the Two Gardens | From A lot to Nothing

Allah, our Creator, shares a beautiful story in His Book, the Holy Quran, which teaches us many lessons. He talks about two friends who were neighbors. One was very wealthy. Allah had given him so much in this world. He had not one but two gardens of grapevines with date palm trees protecting his grapes. He had many other fruits from which he made a lot of money. His garden of fruits would always harvest a crop, and he was never in short supply. Allah also caused a stream of water to flow between his two gardens, giving his gardens all the water they needed. His friend, however, had little in this world of wealth. He neither had wealth nor a garden of fruits.

While the two were talking one day, the wealthy friend told the poor friend, I have more money, fruits, and children than you, and I have a higher status in life than you. Even though everything we have is from Allah, he did not give credit to Allah and was arrogantly showing off. He thought he was better than his poor friend because Allah gave him more in this world. He made his poor friend feel small and bad, which is wrong since Allah does not like that. The wealthy friend said I don't think this garden will ever go away. I don't think there will be a judgment day, and if there is one since God gave me a lot now, He will probably give me even more on judgment day. Allah said in the Holy Quran that the wealthy individual had wronged himself. He did not realize that life is a test, and Allah gives to some people and doesn't give others in this world as a test.

His poor friend was humble and righteous and did not say anything back until he heard his wealthy friend insult Allah. The poor friend told his rich friend he should say MashAllah. He added could you could be so ungrateful to Allah and not thank Him, the One that created you from dust? The poor friend said *Allah is my Master, and I would never associate anyone with God*. The wealthy friend had done wrong because he took credit for everything he had even though Allah had given it. Then the poor friend told him, *even though I have less than you now, perhaps Allah might give me more than you in this world one day or in the afterlife. Possibly Allah might destroy your whole garden, and you'll end up with nothing.*

Later, Allah punished the wealthy friend by destroying both gardens. The rich friend woke up one day seeing his gardens destroyed. He stood there, wringing his hands as he looked at his gardens. Then he felt regret and said, *I wish I had not committed shirk (not giving credit to Allah and being thankful for everything).*

This story teaches us to be careful with money and the beautiful things we have in this world; we should never be ungrateful and think we deserve it without realizing and thanking Allah for all our blessings and gifts. And we should never be arrogant and show off to others, putting them down.

The Story of Cain and Abel | The First Crime Committed on Earth

Because it was the beginning of creation, the laws differed from ours. The children of Prophet Adam and our mother Eve would marry each other but were prohibited from marrying the sibling they were conceived with in the same womb. Our mother, Eve PBUH, fell pregnant 20 times and each time gave birth to twins—a brother and sister.

As Prophet Adam and our mother Eve's children grew older, one of the oldest was Cain (Qabil in Arabic), and one of the younger ones was Abel (Habil in Arabic). The older Cain was not very good-looking, and his younger brother Abel was. Prophet Adam PBUH instructed each brother to marry the other one's sister. Cain's sister was good-looking, and Abel's sister was not. So, Cain felt like he was getting the short end of the stick; not only was he not as good-looking, but he had to marry someone who wasn't very good-looking either. So he refused to marry Abel's sister and wanted to marry his own, conceived within the same womb.

He went to his father, Prophet Adam PBUH, to complain. Prophet Adam PBUH got upset and made dua to Allah. Allah answered by instructing both brothers to sacrifice something for Allah in charity by placing it on a particular mountain. Whoever Allah allows to marry; He would accept their sacrifice by sending fire down to consume it. Since this was the beginning of creation, there were no poor people at the time to give charity, so this was how they would give charity and sacrifice something for Allah.

Abel was a shepherd and brought a good healthy animal to sacrifice and placed it on the mountain. Cain left rotten produce to be sacrificed on the mountain. When they returned, they saw that only the younger brother's sacrifice had been accepted. The older brother's sacrifice was still there and not accepted by Allah, the Glorious.

Instead of Cain pondering why Allah did not accept his sacrifice, he got upset. He told his younger brother that he was going to kill him. His brother was jealous and envious since he was better looking, was going to marry a good-looking girl, and had his sacrifice accepted by Allah. Cain had none of that. Abel responded, saying that Allah only takes from those who are pious, cautious, and fear Allah. He said if you attack me, I will not attack you back.

The Shaytan (devil) taught Cain how to kill, and he struck his brother and killed him. Then he paused, looked at his brother, and realized the Shaytan (devil) had deceived him. He felt regretful. He later returned to his brother's body and saw a crow digging to bury another dead crow. So, he did the same for his brother. Then he grabbed his sister and went to a land far away from his father, Prophet Adam PBUH. They ended up having children, and corruption started to spread from their decedents. Prophet Adam PBUH was distraught that his son had been killed as he loved him very much because he was a soft-hearted righteous son. So, Allah replaced him with another righteous son, Sheath PBUH.

Prophet Job PBUH | What a Great Servant he was to Allah Who Practiced Great Patience

Allah, the Glorious, asks us to ponder the amazing story of Prophet Job (Ayyub in Arabic) PBUH and what a great servant he was: he practiced great patience. His story contains wisdom that people of intelligence can derive and benefit from. Prophet Job PBUH was blessed with a lot in his life. He was good-looking and had a beautiful family with a dozen children and a righteous, loving wife. He also was very wealthy from a good business with many animals, farms, and land. However, the Shaytan (devil) spread rumors around town that Prophet Job PBUH only worshipped Allah because Allah had blessed him with so much. Then Allah, the Glorious, decided to test Prophet Job PBUH to raise his ranks and show people that Prophet Job PBUH was not only worshipping Allah because of his blessings.

Prophet Job PBUH was inflicted with many diseases in his body, and he got extremely ill. His skin was full of blisters and pus. He had leprosy, his skin color changed, and his teeth fell out. His illness was so bad that he had to separate himself from his family. A disease also ruined his land and livestock, and his business started to suffer, resulting in a loss of wealth. His children had an accident, and they all passed away at once.

But Prophet Job PBUH had the exquisite quality of patience, where he never lost his calm. He maintained a good connection with Allah and constantly praised and remembered Allah throughout the day. He remained patient and faithful to His Lord. Even after he was afflicted with his trials and calamities, he never uttered a single word of complaint.

People in the town started to assume that he had committed a major sin. His body had an odor, and the people in the city began to distance themselves from him, except for his wife. She had to take a job to support the two of them. His wife asked him why he didn't ask Allah to cure him and provide what he needed—after all, he is a Prophet of God. He responded that we lived a blessed, wealthy life for 70 years and never complained. I am ashamed to call on my Lord now to remove this hardship. He then asked, *Shouldn't we be thankful for what we were blessed for 70 years?* His wife remained his companion and comforter through the many years of suffering and difficulty.

Then the people of the town decided to stop employing his wife because they thought Prophet Job PBUH was bad luck and blamed everything on him. So Prophet Job and his wife, peace be upon them, started to run out of money and food. One day his wife came with a lot of food, and he asked her where she got it. He noticed that pieces of her hair were missing and realized she was selling her hair to provide for them. He felt terrible and made dua to Allah: *Indeed, the difficulty has touched me, and You are the Most Merciful of the merciful.* Then Allah asked him to kick his foot on the ground, and water from the spring gushed, which he drank. All his blisters, pus, and diseases were cured, and he looked young again.

Allah returned everything to them, and He doubled everything they used to have - and even resurrected their children, blessed them with another twelve children, and made them young again. After everything was restored and multiplied, Prophet Job PBUH knelt and prayed to Allah to express deep gratitude to Him. When his wife returned, she did not recognize him, so she asked if he knew where her husband was.

The Story of Prophet Saleh PBUH | The She-Camel of God That They Killed

God sent one of His Messengers named Saleh PBUH. He was sent to a tribe called *Thamud*. Like the people of Hud, the people of Prophet Saleh PBUH also cultivated rich, prosperous, vibrant, fertile land, led excessively wealthy lives, built grand buildings, and had become vain because of their wealth. Regretfully, with their extravagant lifestyles came the worship of many gods, oppressing the poor, and living a life that went against our Lord's commandments.

Prophet Saleh was a pious, righteous man who held a leadership position in the community, but his call to worship God alone angered many of his people. Prophet Saleh's Message was like all the other Prophets: he warned his people to turn away from worshipping false gods and follow the One God, Allah, who provided everything they had. He advised them to thank their One True Creator and urged the rich to stop oppressing the poor and end all mischief and evil in the land.

The people of Thamud gathered in the shadows of a high mountain, demanding that Prophet Saleh PBUH prove that the One God he spoke of was truly Mighty and Strong. They asked Prophet Saleh PBUH to perform a miracle. They challenged him to produce an incomparable she-camel that must be ten months pregnant, tall and attractive, and emerge from the rock. Prophet Saleh PBUH asked them if a she-camel appeared, would they then believe in his message. They responded yes and prayed with Prophet Saleh PBUH for the miracle to emerge. By the power and will of God, a massive, pregnant she-camel emerged from the rocks at the bottom of the mountain. They saw a powerful, clear sign from their Lord. Several of Prophet Saleh's people believed, yet most continued in disbelief and stubbornness even though they had witnessed a great miracle.

The she-camel lived among the people of Thamud. Later, the people began complaining that the camel drank too much water and frightened other livestock. Prophet Saleh PBUH began to fear for the camel. He warned his people of the great suffering that would befall them if they harmed the she-camel. A group of his people got together and plotted to kill the she-camel. They approached her, shot their arrows, and pierced her with a sword. They cheered and congratulated each other while mocking and laughing at their Prophet PBUH.

Then they challenged Prophet Saleh PBUH to have God punish them for it. The Prophet PBUH warned them that a great punishment would be upon them within three days, hoping his people would realize their mistake and repent for their massive error. Prophet Saleh PBUH and his believers then departed to Palestine to be saved from God's upcoming punishment. Soon, the sky was filled with lightning and thunder, and the Earth shook aggressively with a frightening earthquake or volcanic eruption. No one, including their idols, could save them. In the end, they cried out for mercy, but it was too late.

The Story of Abraham PBUH | Leaving His Family Behind in a Barren Desert Valley

Since Prophet Abraham and his wife Sara, peace be upon them, could not bear any children, Sara asked her husband to marry their servant so they could beget a child before they were too old to raise. Later, Prophet Abraham PBUH was commanded by God to take both his second wife Hagar and their son Ismael and leave them in a barren desert valley. As soon as Prophet Abraham PBUH started to leave, Hagar cried out, *Where are you going? Why are you leaving us?* Prophet Abraham PBUH did not respond. After a few more attempts to find answers, Hagar asked if this was a commandment from God. He responded, *Yes.* She replied, *If God commanded you to leave us, then leave us because God would never leave us to perish.* Despite being in the middle of a desert valley, she was sure that God would not abandon her and her child. He left them with little water and some dates. Later, Hagar ran out of food and water and started to worry. She climbed Mount Safa hill, crying out, *Is anyone there?* Then she ran to another mountain called Mount Marwa, again crying out, *Is anyone there?* She paced back and forth to each hill seven times.

On the seventh round, Hajar saw Angel Gabriel descend from the sky and strike the ground with his wing, causing water to gush upward from the Earth. This water is now referred to as Zam Zam water. Angel Gabriel declared, *Zam, Zam,* meaning *stop, stop,* commanding the water to stop. This well to this today nourishes pilgrims of Mecca every day. Hagar and her child were then rescued. Years later, when Ismael grew into a man, his father, Prophet Abraham PBUH, returned and built the house in Mecca called the Kaaba.

The Sabbath-Breakers | Those Who Fished on the Day of the Sabbath—the Forbidden Day to Fish

Allah, the Glorious, shares a story in the Holy Quran about a group of people who lived before us. The Children of Israel lived in a village by the sea and made their livelihood from fishing. They were disobeying God, so God sent them a test where He instructed them not to fish or work on the day of the Sabbath (i.e., Saturday), but they were allowed to fish on the other days of the week. God, the Almighty, tested them by not having any fish in the sea all week; on the day of the Sabbath, many fish would come out. There would be so many that they could see them jump out of the water.

Some of the children of Israel thought of a trick. They decided not to fish or set their net on the day of the Sabbath as instructed. Instead, they put out their nets the night before on Friday and returned the day after the Sabbath to collect all the fish in the net. When they returned the day after the Sabbath, they found a lot of fish in their net and took them home. They thought they were clever and tricking Allah, but they were only tricking themselves. The people in the town smelled the fish cooking from their home and asked them where they had gotten all the fish, so they told them of their trick and deception. Some people in the village copied what they had done, and some did not.

At that moment, those who did not fish broke into two different groups. One was the best: those who did not fish and spoke up against those who did, warning them to fear Allah and stop what they were doing. The second group, those who did not fish, did not speak up and forbid those who did, allowing the disobedience to continue. Even though they did not fish on the forbidden day, they did not speak up against those who did fish. They would tell those that did speak up and preach to mind their own business and ask, 'why do you preach to those whom Allah is about to destroy with a severe punishment?' The preachers would respond *so that we can be free from guilt and perhaps fear Allah, stop what they are doing, regret what they have done, and be saved from the punishment of Allah.* Allah has commanded us to enjoin what is good and forbid what is evil.

One day, Allah brought down his punishment and turned those who fished on the day of the Sabbath into monkeys and apes for three days; then, they vanished. He also turned and vanished those who did not fish but did not speak up against those who did because they let the sinners sin. The only group saved were those who did not fish and spoke up, prohibiting those who fished. The ones saved saw them as monkeys and asked them, *Didn't we forbid you from doing this?*

The Story of Prophet Hud PBUH | Arrogant People Went from Strength to Nothing

Prophet Hud (Eber in English) PBUH was sent to an ancient tribe called Ad, believed to have been in the curved sand hills of Oman and Yemen. They worshiped idols as gods, which they thought would give them happiness and money and protect them from evil, harm, and disasters.

The people of Prophet Hud were very tall, strong, and well built. They were arrogant people who would show off, bully, and oppress others with their large size. According to the Holy Quran, they would say, ***Who is greater than us in strength? (Quran 41:15)*** They were known to build tall towers. Their area became known as the land of a thousand pillars since God blessed them with fertile soil, abundant agriculture, many children, an ample supply of livestock, and easy access to water resources. They mistakenly understood the purpose of life was to gather wealth, status in life, and live in luxury.

Prophet Hud PBUH would command them to fear and obey God. According to the Holy Quran, Prophet Hud PBUH would say to his people: *...O my people, worship Allah; you have no god besides Him. You are not but inventors [of falsehood] (Quran 11:50).* Prophet Hud PBUH advised them to ask God for forgiveness for their arrogance and carelessness and told them that if they sought forgiveness, God would increase their power, strength, and wealth.

However, the people of Prophet Hud PBUH proudly saw themselves as the most powerful nation. They rejected their Prophet's Message, believing their bodies would decay to dust and be swept away by the wind after death. With their hearts and minds filled with the accumulation of this world, they would ask their Prophet, *Why did God choose you when you are no different from the rest of us? You eat and drink like the rest of us.* Prophet Hud's people proudly stated, *Have you come to turn us away from our gods? Then bring the disaster you threaten us with if we don't listen!* Prophet Hud PBUH turned to God the Almighty and renounced his people.

Soon after, the people of Hud suffered a three-year famine and a drought that spread throughout the once green, fertile, and abundant land. The people looked to the sky, hoping to see signs of rain. One fateful day the weather changed. The burning heat changed to furious violent winds, which God the Almighty imposed for seven nights and eight days. The winds ripped apart their homes, possessions, clothing, and even the skin on their bodies. The sands of the desert swallowed and buried their crops. Only Prophet Hud PBUH and his small group of believers were saved and believed to have migrated to Southern Yemen.

The Story of Prophet Moses PBUH | The Arrogant & Oppressive Pharaoh and The Escape from Egypt

The Pharaoh who ruled in the time of Prophet Moses PBUH was a very arrogant, oppressive tyrant who would declare to be god and slaughter newborn sons because he was afraid a boy might grow up and destroy his kingdom. When Prophet Moses BUH was born, his mother was distraught that the oppressive Pharaoh was going to slaughter her baby, but Allah, the Glorious, inspired her to make a wooden box, place him in it, and cast him into the river without fearing or grieving because He would indeed return him to her and make him one of His Messengers.

The palace servants found the basket with Prophet Moses PBUH as a baby. They took it to the Pharaoh and his wife Asiya, who, unlike her husband, was a very pious and righteous woman. She said to the Pharaoh, *He will be the comfort of our eye for me and you. Do not kill him; perhaps he may benefit us, or we may adopt him as a son.* She was not able to have a baby on her own. So, they took him, and she built a special love for this baby. Allah saved Prophet Moses PBUH when he was a baby, and he was never harmed.

As Prophet Moses PBUH got older, Allah blessed him with good judgment, knowledge, health, strength, and wisdom. Before he was a Prophet, Moses PBUH saw two men fighting. One was an Israelite, and the other was an Egyptian. The Egyptian was beating up the Israelite. Once Prophet Moses PBUH saw this, he got angry and immediately struck the Egyptian, who died on the spot. Realizing that he had accidentally killed someone without meaning to do so, he felt regret. He begged Allah for forgiveness, and Allah forgave him.

When Prophet Moses PBUH realized that the chief was looking to trail and kill him, he escaped from Egypt quickly without taking anything with him. As he fled, he sat under shade and saw a band of shepherds watering their sheep while two sisters struggled to keep their animals from running to the lake to drink. Prophet Musa PBUH walked up to them, asking them what the matter was and why they weren't letting their animals drink like the rest. They replied they wanted to wait until the men were finished feeding their animals water before feeding theirs because they didn't want to mix with the men and their father was too old to do it.

Prophet Musa PBUH wanted to make up for his mistake in Egypt by doing good deeds. Prophet Musa PBUH voluntarily took their animals and went down to the lake to feed the two sister's animals. Then he returned the animals to the sisters and started to walk over to a tree for shade.

Under the tree, he made a dua to Allah, asking Allah to send him whatever good his way, that he would be grateful as he is poor and has nothing. Afterward, the young ladies returned home earlier than usual, surprising their father. After their father heard what had happened, he asked his daughters to invite him over to thank him for his actions. The girl he had helped came back shyly and told Prophet Musa PBUH that her father wanted to thank him for his actions. So, he went. One of the daughters suggested to her father that he should employ Prophet Moses PBUH as he was strong and trustworthy, and they could use his help. Her father offered Prophet Moses PBUH a job and food and even married his daughter to him. After ten years, Prophet Moses PBUH decided to return to Egypt with his family.

The Story of Prophet Jesus PBUH | The Attempt to Crucify Prophet Jesus PBUH

The mother of Prophet Jesus PBUH is Mary (Mariam in Arabic). She was a very pious and righteous woman, the holiest and greatest of all women who ever lived. Mary PBUH gave birth to Prophet Jesus PBUH in the valley of Bethlehem, away from the people, after which she returned. Prophet Jesus PBUH performed a miracle by speaking as a baby by the power and will of God. God created Jesus Christ without a human father, just as Prophet Adam PBUH was born without a father or mother; Allah said Be, and it Was.

As Jesus Christ grew into adulthood, he began to travel and preach God's message throughout the land of Palestine to the children of Israel. He taught the Book God sent him, known as the Injeel. To prove to the people that he was a Prophet of God, God granted Prophet Jesus PBUH the ability to perform miracles. He was able to fashion birds from clay by blowing into them, turning them into real birds. He was also able to heal the sick and the blind and even resurrect the dead, all by the will and power of God the Almighty. Prophet Jesus PBUH preached and stressed that no deity is worthy of worship except the one true God, and only through God can one obtain salvation in the hereafter. Prophet Jesus PBUH attracted an inner circle of devoted followers who listened to his teachings with humility. They became known as disciples.

Because the Children of Israel had gone away from the straight path of God, Allah, the Glorious, sent them their final Prophet, Jesus Christ, to remind them that this was their last chance to fulfill God's commandments. When Jesus Christ continued to preach God's message, commanding them to do and avoid certain things, they got frustrated instead of believing and following him. They turned their backs on him, rejected him, and even plotted against him.

The children of Israel complained to the Roman authorities, who were pagan idol worshipers with political power at the time. The Children of Israel complained that Prophet Jesus PBUH was preaching something new. They provoked the Romans to rise against Prophet Jesus PBUH, making the Roman governor believe that the call of Jesus Christ conveyed direct threats against Roman power. The Roman governor ordered that Prophet Jesus PBUH be arrested, then crucified by hanging him on a cross and starving him - a common form of shame killing.

The Israelites and the Roman authorities never could harm, crucify, or kill Prophet Jesus PBUH. The Romans crucified someone else, thinking it was Prophet Jesus PBUH. God ended up rescuing His Prophet by raising Prophet Jesus' soul and body to save him.

The Story of Prophet Muhammad PBUH | God Sends His Last Messenger and Prophet to Us

Muhammad PBUH was born about 570 years after the birth of Prophet Jesus PBUH. He was born in Mecca, in the Arabian Peninsula. The people of Mecca were devoted idol-worshippers, and the area and period at the time were full of ignorance, foolishness, and misguidance. There were many idols in Mecca, and that was wrong.

After God sent many Prophets and Messengers, he sent his final Messenger to us, Prophet Muhammad PBUH. At forty, Prophet Muhammad PBUH received his first Revelation from God via the Angel Gabriel in a cave. Prophet Muhammad PBUH spent the remaining portion of his life explaining and living the teachings of the Holy Quran and Islam, the religion God had revealed to us.

Although he was known among his community as *the truthful and the trustworthy*, *most* people did not believe him or his message. Soon after, a massive campaign started, persecuting those who believed in the message. After thirteen years of preaching in Mecca, Prophet Muhamad PBUH migrated to the city of Medina, where he gained followers. These followers made him the leader of the town.

The idol-worshippers of Mecca plotted and attempted to attack those who believed in God's message. However, what was originally a small group of Muslims grew in number, and they could withstand the attack of the idol-worshippers of Mecca. Within ten years, the Prophet PBUH led an army back to Mecca and conquered it in a bloodless victory. Later, Islam spread throughout the World. God states in the Holy Quran that He did not send Prophet Muhammad PBUH except as a mercy for humanity.

The End.

Printed in France by Amazon
Brétigny-sur-Orge, FR